A typical example of a 4¹/₂ litre with Vanden Plas open-tourer body, the closest to standard coachwork offered on the vintage Bentley. This very original car was delivered in December 1929.

THE BENTLEY

Nick Georgano

Shire Publications Ltd

CONTENTS

Printed in Great Britain by C. I. Thomas & Sons (Haverfordwest) Ltd, Press Buildings, Merlins Bridge, Haverfordwest, Dyfed SA61 1XF.

British Library Cataloguing in Publication Data: Georgano, G. N. Bentley. — (Shire Albums; No. 292). I. Title. II. Series. 629.222. ISBN 0-7478-0192-4.

Editorial Consultant: Michael E. Ware, Curator of the National Motor Museum, Beaulieu.

Cover: *A 1930 Bentley Speed Six, with Vanden Plas replica body, chassis number 2755, owned by Jack Smith.*

ACKNOWLEDGEMENTS
I would like to thank Bill Boddy for help with photograph captioning and Jack Smith for the loan of several books and allowing me to photograph his Speed Six.
    All photographs are from the National Motor Museum Photographic Library, with the following exceptions: pages 30 (bottom), 31 and 32, which are reproduced by courtesy of Rolls-Royce Motors Ltd; pages 18 (top), 23 (bottom), 25 (bottom) and the front cover, which are by the author.

A handsome coupé on a 3 litre chassis. The date is not certain, but front-wheel brakes indicate that it is of 1924 or later.

2

W. O. Bentley at the wheel of a 12/15 hp DFP in 1914. Note the stoneguard protecting the vee radiator. Bentley had many successes in sprints, hillclimbs and races in DFP cars between 1912 and 1914.

THE VINTAGE YEARS

It is a curious coincidence that the makers of two of Britain's most famous cars, Henry Royce and Walter Owen Bentley, should have begun their careers as railway engineering apprentices, Royce with the Great Northern Railway at Peterborough, and Bentley in the same company's shops at Doncaster. The parallel ends there, though, for while Royce came from a very poor background and had to cut short his apprenticeship because his aunt could no longer afford the £20 annual premium, Bentley's family were comfortably off. His father was a businessman and they lived in Avenue Road, St John's Wood, in London. His youthful enthusiasms were cricket and motorcycling (he raced a 5 horsepower Rex at Brooklands in 1909), and in 1910 he bought his first car, a Riley V-twin two-seater. He subsequently owned two Sizaire-Naudins, a single-cylinder model and then a four. He had a high regard for this make.

After his time at Doncaster, when he worked under Henry Ivatt, designer of the 4-4-2 Atlantic locomotives, he was a General Assistant at the National Motor Cab Company in Hammersmith, then in 1912 joined his brother H. M. Bentley in selling French DFP cars. They were not particularly fast, but Bentley soon improved their performance by using lighter pistons made from 12 per cent copper and 88 per cent aluminium. Thus equipped, Bentley's DFPs won several races at Brooklands and, with a new Bentley-designed camshaft, took Class B records in 1913 and 1914. His time for a flying mile was 89.7 mph (144 km/h), a creditable figure for a 2 litre car. The Bentley brothers persuaded DFP to adopt aluminium pistons in a production car, which they sold as the 12/40, though not many were made as they were launched less than a year before the outbreak of the First World War.

3

The third prototype, chassis number EXP 3, commonly known as 'The Cab' because of its all-weather body by Harrison. It had the first 9 foot 9¹/₂ inch (2985 mm) chassis, as the first two prototypes were shorter, at 9 feet 4 inches (2840 mm). It was photographed by the King Alfred statue in Winchester in 1920.

During the war Bentley worked for the Technical Board of the Royal Naval Air Service to improve the French Clerget rotary engine, where his experience with aluminium pistons was of great value. He worked first at Gwynne's Engineering of Hammersmith, who were to make a quality light car after the war, and then at Humber in Coventry. The modified Clerget designs bore his name, being called the BR1 and BR2 (Bentley Rotary).

After the war Bentley returned to the partnership of Bentley and Bentley, whose business as before was the importation of the DFP. However, his ambition was to see a car bearing his own name and in August 1919 he formed Bentley Motors Ltd, a successor to another company of the same name which was concerned with sales. Nominal share capital was £200,000, but cash in the bank was only £18,575. The company was undercapitalised from the start, and a mortgage was taken out to finance the building of a factory at Cricklewood in north-west London. The first prototypes were not made there, but at New Street Mews, off Baker Street. This property belonged to J. H. Easter, who did body trimming for the DFPs.

Bentley's right-hand man was Frank Burgess, a former designer and works driver for Humber, who had been responsible for the twin-overhead-camshaft engine used in that company's 1914 Tourist Trophy racing cars. This engine was itself closely based on Ernest Henry's design for the 1912 Grand Prix Peugeots. Burgess brought a TT Humber to Bentley Motors, and some chassis features were reflected in the new Bentley. The engine, however, had only a single camshaft, driven by shaft from the front of the crankshaft. There were four valves per cylinder, a Peugeot feature, and the dimensions were 80 by 149 mm (about 3¹/₈ by 5⁷/₈ inches), a long stroke even for those days. At 2996 cc, capacity was just under 3 litres, and the car was christened the 3 litre model. This was the first time that a British car had been described in litres, and this puzzled many motorists who were used to horsepower. However the RAC horsepower rating of 15.9 would have made the engine seem smaller than it was, for the rating system was calculated on the bore and took no account of the Bentley's unusually long stroke.

The rest of the car was conventional, with a four-speed gearbox controlled by a right-hand gear lever, semi-elliptic leaf springs all round and brakes on the rear wheels only (until 1924). It was announced in *The Autocar* in May 1919, the description being accompanied by a drawing by the well-known artist F. Gordon Crosby, as no car existed in the metal. Bentley described the kind of car he had in mind and gave Crosby a free hand in the drawing. The radiator was more pointed than in the actual car (more like a DFP), but the famous winged B was similar to that which was adopted.

A chassis was shown at London's first

A 3 litre with typical open four-seater bodywork, taking part in the Nidderdale Trial in November 1950. The chassis is number 76, delivered in June 1922.

postwar Motor Show, in October 1919, but it was a non-runner; among its drawbacks was the rather serious one of having no crankshaft. The starting handle was pinned on to an empty crankcase, and the flywheel supported by a stub shaft a few inches long. An engine was running at New Street Mews by Christmas (causing an irate matron of a nearby nursing home to complain at the noise), and deliveries were promised for June 1920. However, development work took longer than anticipated, and the first car was not delivered to a customer until September

1921. It was a two-door saloon and went to a friend of W. O., Noel van Raalte. He paid £1150 for the chassis, quite an increase on the £750 quoted in the original 1919 announcement.

Once production started at Cricklewood, the cars soon lived up to the promise of their original announcement, and those buyers who were patient enough to wait for more than two years were mostly well satisfied. 21 were delivered in 1921, and production reached 122 in 1922, 204 in 1923 and 402 in 1924. This was very close to the peak year of 1928, when 408

A stripped 3 litre driven by May Cunliffe at a sand race at Southport in August 1927.

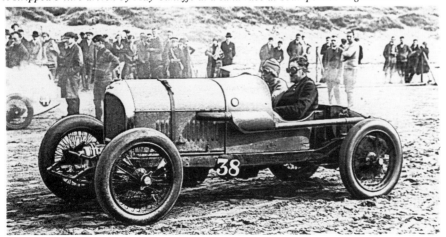

5

Bentleys with more formal coachwork were frequent winners at the Concours d'Elégance so popular between the wars. This 6½ litre saloon took second prize at the 1928 Southport Rally.

An interesting car which began as the second experimental 6½ litre with a tourer body and was then given this angular saloon body which earned it the nickname 'The Box'. W. O. used it as his personal car for several years, and it was fitted with the first prototype 8 litre engine.

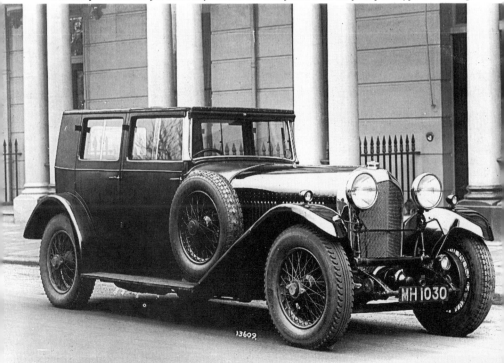

cars were delivered. By the middle of the decade the name Bentley had already acquired the mystique which has lasted up to the present day. Racing successes ensured that the layman knew more of Bentley than of any other sporting make, while well-known figures such as Prince George, later the Duke of Kent, and the actresses Gertrude Lawrence and Beatrice Lillie were also among Bentley customers.

Bentley did not have a coachworking department, but there were some virtually standard bodies which were recommended by the makers. The open four-seater tourers were mostly made by Vanden Plas, whose premises were close to Cricklewood. Other coachbuilders were soon asked to work on the 3 litre chassis, and a variety of styles was seen, from stark open two-seaters to heavy landaulettes. W. O. never anticipated that his cars would carry formal closed coachwork, but customers had to be satisfied, and to meet the need a longer chassis was listed from 1923. Three basic types of 3 litre were made, commonly identified by the colour of their badges. They can be summarised as follows:

Blue Label. The standard model with 9 foot 9½ inch (2985 mm) wheelbase, made from 1921 to 1929, together with a 10 foot 10 inch (3302 mm) model made from 1923 to 1929. Total production, 1013.

Red Label. The 9 foot 9½ inch model with higher compression ratio (5.3:1) made from 1924 to 1929. Total production, 582 (including 71 TT replicas).

Green Label. Extra short wheelbase, 9 foot 0 inch (2743 mm), with 6.3:1 compression ratio. Guaranteed 100 mph (160 km/h) top speed. Made from 1924 to 1926. Total production, 18.

Of the 1613 3 litres made, some 670 are known to survive today.

Although Bentley saw his cars primarily as fast tourers, the demand for closed coachwork made him realise that more power was needed. At first he considered a six-cylinder engine on the same lines as the 3 litre, giving a capacity of just under 4½ litres, but a chance encounter with the prototype Rolls-Royce Phantom 1 in France convinced him that an even larger engine was needed, and the six-cylinder car ended up with dimensions of 100 by 140 mm, giving a capacity of 6597 cc. The chassis differed in a number of respects from that of the 3 litre; the cone clutch was replaced by a plate clutch, the differential was much heavier and four-wheel brakes were used from the start. The brake drums were finned as opposed to the plain variety used on the four-cylinder Bentleys. The chief difference in engine design was that the camshaft drive was by three-throw coupled rod rather than the vertical shaft of the smaller model. The 6½ was offered in three wheelbase lengths: 132, 144 and 150 inches (3353, 3658 and 3810 mm). The longest made for an enormous car, 16 feet 7 inches (5055 mm) long, or as large as a Rolls-Royce Phantom 1 or Daimler 45 hp, and at £1450 for a chassis it was not much cheaper than those models. The finest coachbuilders in the land, such as Barker and Hooper, built magnificent bodies on the 6½ litre.

In 1928 came a sporting version known as the Speed Six. This was recognisable by the radiator, which had parallel sides in contrast to that of the standard 6½ which tapered towards the bottom. A higher compression ratio and twin carburetters raised power from 147 to 160 brake horsepower (bhp). The Speed Six was probably the most successful Bentley in racing, with two consecutive Le Mans victories, but it also carried formal coachwork. Two Speed Sixes were used as patrol cars by the Criminal Investigation Department of the Western Australia Police Force, surely the only Bentley police cars in the world. Carrying locally made Bolton saloon bodies, they served from 1930 to 1947; when they were withdrawn from service it was said: 'There has hardly been a major crime committed in this State which has not been affected by one or other of the Bentleys.'

Although preceded by the 4½ litre, it is logical to deal with the 8 litre next, as it was part of the six-cylinder family. W. O. firmly believed that there was no substitute for litres and far preferred to

One of the last 8 litres, delivered in June 1932, this carries a saloon body by H. J. Mulliner.

enlarge an engine than to supercharge a smaller one — witness his dislike of the blower 4¹/₂. The 8 litre's engine was essentially that of the 6¹/₂ with bore increased to 110 mm, giving a capacity of 7982 cc. Output was 200 or 225 bhp according to compression ratio. Two wheelbases were available, the longest being even longer than the 6¹/₂ at 13 feet (3962 mm). Nevertheless, an 8 litre could exceed 100 mph (160 km/h) unless fitted with too heavy a body. These were as varied as on any other Bentley chassis: saloons, limousines, coupés, at least one

The only Cricklewood Bentley not to have an overhead-camshaft engine was the 4 litre, built as an emergency measure to provide the company with a cheaper car than the 8 litre. Designed by Sir Harry Ricardo, its engine used the inlet-over-exhaust layout and gave about 120 bhp. Unfairly castigated by some Bentley enthusiasts, its fault lay in its heavy chassis, similar to that of the 8 litre, but with a light body it performed well, and at least one current owner rates his as livelier than his 4¹/₂. This one carries a drophead coupé body by Freestone & Webb.

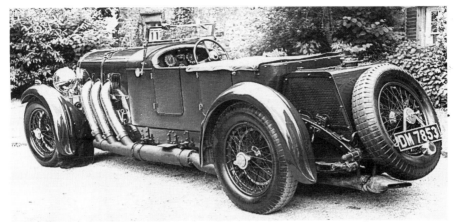

Described as 'the only boy racer 8 litre built by the works', this remarkable car has a very narrow fabric Vanden Plas body, high-compression pistons, lightened flywheel and twin Bosch magnetos. It was built to the order of Captain Vivian Hewitt, who covered only 6500 miles (10,500 km) in it. It is now in the collection of the Honourable Alan Clark.

sedanca de ville, and a few open tourers. One fortunate family, the Bustards, had two 8 litres, a Freestone & Webb saloon and a Thrupp & Maberly limousine. The latter cost £3055, just about the top price for any vintage Bentley.

The 8 litre could not have come at a worse time, being introduced in 1930, when the depression was hitting particularly hard at expensive cars, and Bentley Motors Ltd was only eight months away from receivership. Only 67 of the one hundred 8 litre chassis were sold by the company while it was still independent,

A 4¹/₂ litre with Maythorn coupé body. Originally this chassis carried an open Vanden Plas body. With a delivery date of February 1931, it is one of the last 4¹/₂s.

Charles Amherst Villiers, designer of the Bentley supercharger, at the wheel of his own Blower 4½, photographed in the 1950s.

the remaining 33 being completed under the direction of the receiver.

While the 6½ litre was catering well for the luxury market, W. O. needed a new sports car if he was to remain competitive in the late 1920s. The answer was the 4½ litre, a four-cylinder car with the same dimensions as the 6½, and using many components such as transmission, frame and brakes from the 3 litre. Capacity was 4398 cc and output around 110 bhp, so with a light four-seater body the 4½ could exceed 90 mph (145 km/h). It was available in two wheelbase lengths, the standard 10 feet 10 inches, and a special short version at 9 feet 9½ inches, of which only nine were delivered new, though quite a number of standard chassis have been shortened over the years. When they were new, most customers wanted the long chassis, to W. O.'s regret, and many carried fairly formal saloon bodies. The nearest to standard coachwork on a 4½ was the four-seater open tourer by Vanden Plas. Among builders of saloon and coupé bodies were Hooper, Maythorn, Gurney Nutting, H. J. Mulliner and Windover. The Prince of Wales had a very special four-door saloon from Gurney Nutting, with raised window sills, interior-operated spot lamps, semaphore indicators (very rare in 1928) and lockers for his golf clubs.

THE BLOWER BENTLEYS

The most controversial variant of the 4½ litre was the supercharged model, or 'Blower 4½' as it is commonly known. This came about because Sir Henry Birkin, who had finished second at Le Mans in 1928 with a standard 4½, realised that more power would be needed if the company were to repeat the success in 1929. A 4½ litre belonging to Bernard Rubin was taken to Birkin's workshop in Welwyn Garden City and fitted with a Roots-type supercharger designed by Amherst Villiers, then Britain's leading expert on forced induction. There is some mystery about the early work on the Blower Bentley, and it is likely that initial work took place at the Cricklewood factory. However, W. O.'s known dislike of supercharging ('it would pervert its design and corrupt its performance', he said) meant that extensive work on supercharging would

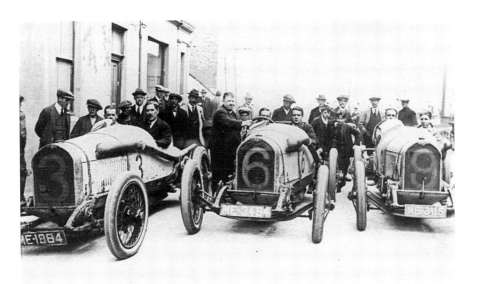

The Bentley team for the 1922 Tourist Trophy in the Isle of Man. They had higher compression ratios than standard, and the flat radiators were unlike those of any other Bentley. It was said that the modifications cost no more than £25 per car; the flat radiators represented a saving, as the traditional pointed radiator was expensive to make.

not be welcome at Cricklewood. The competition cars were prepared at Welwyn, but the run of fifty production blown cars was made at Cricklewood, owing to Woolf Barnato's support for the idea.

The blower more than doubled the output of the 4½ litre engine, to 240 bhp, but the cars were never very reliable in racing. Its first race was typical: in the Brooklands Six Hours of 1929, Birkin led the field from the start but then retired. The team cars never won a race, though Birkin finished a remarkable second at the 1930 French Grand Prix in a stripped four-seater tourer. He was beaten only by Philippe Etancelin's Grand Prix Bugatti Type 35 and was ahead of several other Bugattis. There is some evidence that, had the blown cars been more successful, W. O. might have modified his hostile stance, for the regular 4½s from mid 1929 onwards had heavier crankshafts. These were necessary for a supercharged engine, but not for the standard engine, which never suffered from bottom-end weakness.

RACING WITH THE BENTLEY BOYS

The first appearance of a Bentley in racing took place four months before the car went on sale. In May 1921 Frank Clement won the Junior Sprint Handicap at Brooklands at 72.5 mph (117 km/h). The following year a team of three cars was prepared for the Tourist Trophy and one for the Indianapolis 500 Mile race. They had flat radiators quite unlike those of any other Bentleys, and higher compression engines. W. B. Hawkes could manage no higher than thirteenth at Indianapolis, though this was quite creditable for a modified sports car competing against purpose-built racing cars. In the TT Bentleys finished second (Clement), fourth (Bentley) and fifth (Hawkes). It was W. O.'s last race as a driver, though he acted as Birkin's mechanic in the 1929 TT.

The Bentley name is inseparably linked with Le Mans, and the marque was there for the first 24 Hour Race in June 1923. John Duff entered a car privately and finished fourth. W. O. was not in favour of the race at first: 'I think the whole thing's crazy

11

The lone 3 litre which W. B. Hawkes drove to thirteenth place at the 1922 Indianapolis 500 Mile Race. Like the TT cars, it had a body by Ewart (of gas-geyser fame).

— nobody will finish. Cars are not meant to stand that sort of strain for 24 hours.' The following year Duff won, the first of five Bentley victories on the Sarthe circuit. In 1925 there were works entries for the first time, but both cars retired, as they did in 1926. In 1927 they redeemed themselves with one of the epic drives in motor-racing history. A multiple crash at White House Corner eliminated two of the three Bentleys and severely damaged the third, but S. C. H. (Sammy) Davis and Dr Dudley Benjafield nursed it though to victory.

Davis and Benjafield were just two of the group of drivers who were known as the Bentley Boys. The others included the

Bentley's third consecutive (and fourth overall) Le Mans win came in 1929 when Birkin and Barnato drove the Speed Six 'Old Number One' to victory, ahead of three other Bentleys. Birkin is seen here, with Jack Dunfee in the second-place 4$^{1}/_{2}$ litre behind him.

Three supercharged 4¹/₂s were entered at Le Mans in 1930, but none finished. This is Dr Benjafield in Number 8 which retired with a collapsed piston after completing twenty of the 24 hours. The race was won by Barnato and Kidston in a Speed Six.

millionaire all-round sportsman Woolf Barnato, who became chairman when he rescued the company from financial disaster in 1925, the brothers Clive and Jack Dunfee, Glen Kidston, Bernard Rubin, Jean Chassagne and Sir Henry Birkin. Between them they dominated Le Mans from 1928 to 1930, Barnato/Rubin winning in 1928 in a 4¹/₂, Barnato/Birkin in 1929 in a Speed Six and Barnato/Kidston in 1930, again in a Speed Six. Among numerous Brooklands successes were wins in the 1929 Six Hours and 500 Mile races and the 1930 Double Twelve Hours. The blower Bentley never won a race, but Birkin took the Brooklands Outer Circuit Lap Record in 1931 at 137.96 mph (222 km/h).

A fine picture of a Speed Six at Brooklands; the Sammy Davis/Clive Dunfee car in the 1930 Double Twelve in which they finished second at an average of 85.68 mph (138 km/h).

Vanden Plas built bodies for many of the open 3½ and 4¼ litre Bentleys, including this 1934 3½ seen at a postwar hillclimb, part of the 1953 Morecambe rally.

A 1934 3½ litre with Barker drophead body built for Prince Ali Khan, in use as an official car at Brooklands. On the left is Junior Car Club secretary 'Bunny' Dyer and on the right is official scrutineer Hugh P. McConnell.

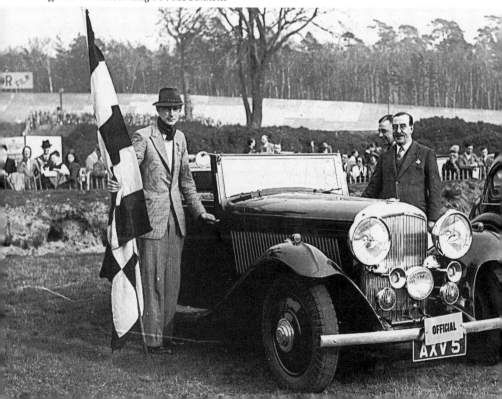

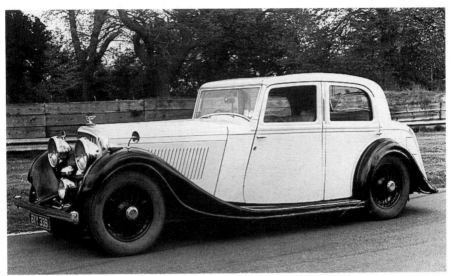

A Thrupp & Maberly saloon on a 1935 3¹/₂ litre chassis. It is not unlike the more familiar Park Ward saloon, which was made in larger numbers.

THE SILENT SPORTS CAR

The Bentley company was seriously undercapitalised from the start and would probably have collapsed without Barnato's intervention in 1925. This was effectively a takeover, for Barnato held 109,400 £1 preference shares and 114,000 one shilling ordinary shares. In contrast W. O. held six thousand and three thousand shares respectively, though his brother H. M. Bentley and one or two others also had some stake in the company. In June 1931 the company's debts were such that it could no longer continue trading; Barnato's fortune had been eroded by the Depression and he was no longer willing to support Bentley. A receiver was appointed, and it was expected that Napier would acquire Bentley, especially as W. O. had been having discussions with the Acton company about a new twin-overhead-camshaft sports car. However, they were outbid to the tune of £20,481 by a mystery group called the British Central Equitable Trust Ltd. They were acting for an unknown company, and Bentley learnt only several days later (from cocktail party conversation overheard by

his wife) that the company was Rolls-Royce.

A new firm was formed, Bentley Motors (1931) Ltd, which was a wholly owned subsidiary of Rolls-Royce. W. O. was retained as an employee, but he had little say in the design of the new car that bore his name. Increasingly unhappy, he left when his contract came up for renewal in 1935, joining Lagonda, for whom he designed the LG6 and V12. He was also responsible for the 2¹/₂ litre twin-overhead-camshaft six which powered the postwar Lagonda and went into the Aston Martin DB2. He died in 1971, by which time he was a revered figure to the Bentley Drivers' Club, welcoming many gatherings of the vintage cars at his home in Surrey.

In the summer of 1933 the new Bentley was announced. Known as the 3¹/₂ litre, it had a modified Rolls-Royce 20/25 engine in a new chassis which had been designed for a 2¹/₂ litre Rolls-Royce that never went into production. The 3669 cc pushrod overhead-valve six-cylinder engine had a higher compression ratio than

An appropriate location for a 1937 4¹/₄ with classic Vanden Plas tourer body.

in the 20/25, twin carburetters and improved cylinder-head design. Output was about 105 bhp, 20 bhp more than the unit used in the Rolls. The chassis was conventional, with semi-elliptic springs all round, and brakes assisted by an engine-driven servo. The four-speed gearbox had synchromesh on the two upper ratios only.

In the Rolls-Royce tradition, only chassis were supplied, but the makers recommended a number of styles which were made in small runs by the coachbuilders. This cut costs considerably, and also the waiting time for delivery. The best-known of these recommended bodies were the open sports tourer by Vanden Plas and the four-door saloon by Park Ward. At the 1933 London Motor Show examples of these were priced at £1380 and £1460 respectively (there were no exact prices

The parallel opening door was patented by A. H. Pass of dealers Pass & Joyce. At least two bodies were made by James Young, one with the parallel door on the near side, the other with it on the off side, as here. The chassis is a 1937 4¹/₄ litre.

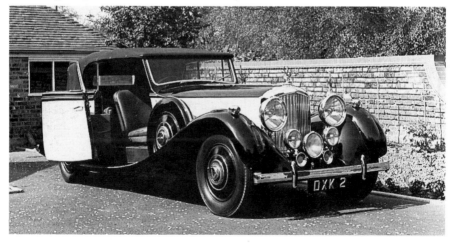

An unusual body built for the Marquess of Cholmondeley, probably to his own design, by Van Vooren on a 1936 3½ litre chassis.

as these varied according to detailed equipment). Delivery could be almost immediate. By contrast an individually designed custom body might cost up to £800, to which had to be added a chassis price of £1100. If such a body were ordered by the customer, construction might take up to six months, though sometimes the more exotic custom styles were built by the coachbuilders for the motor shows and could be bought straight off the stand.

The new Bentley, or Rolls-Bentley as it was dubbed by the popular press, was a much smoother and more comfortable car than the old-school models, and very little slower than a 4½ over twisting roads. It may have disappointed the purists who worshipped the vintage models with their burbling exhausts and outside gearchange, but all those who could afford the new

An attractive airline saloon by Barker on a 1935 3½ litre chassis, supplied to the Marquesa de Portago, mother of the 1950s Spanish racing driver who was killed in the 1957 Mille Miglia.

Built for the 1938 London Show, this was a two-seater coupé by Park Ward, with many extra features such as electric window lifts (very rare at this time) and rear blind, and a fitted fire extinguisher. Charlie Ward was said to have been inspired by the Mercedes-Benz 540K coupé when he styled this car. Nicknamed 'the honeymoon express', it sold for £1800.

Bentleys were happy to do so. Even W. O. said of the new car: 'Taking all things into consideration, I would rather own this Bentley than any car produced under that name.' The vintage models became the province of the younger and less wealthy enthusiasts who formed the backbone of the Vintage Sports Car Club when it was formed in 1934, and the Bentley Drivers' Club in 1936. By then a ten-year old 3 litre could be had for anything from £40 to £100. Two years later the

official cash price to the trade of a Speed Six was between £5 and £10, according to the year of manufacture!

Among those who appreciated the new Bentleys were the racing drivers Raymond Mays and Eddie Hall (who had four each), Malcolm Campbell, Billy Cotton, George Eyston and Woolf Barnato. Owners from other motor companies included R. Gordon Sutherland of Aston Martin, Leonard Lord of Austin, David Brown and Archie Frazer Nash.

Also built on the Mark V chassis were two Corniche saloons. Intended as 1940 models, they had Van Vooren bodies styled by Ivan Evernden and Georges Paulin. One wonders if there would have been some sales resistance to the absence of a traditional Bentley radiator grille.

Known as the Embiricos Bentley, this is a 1939 4¹/₄ litre with streamlined body designed by Georges Paulin and built in Paris by Pourtout for the Greek driver A. M. Embiricos. A modified engine and higher axle ratio gave it a top speed of over 120 mph (193 km/h), and it averaged 114 mph (183 km/h) in an hour at Brooklands. In 1949 it finished sixth at Le Mans.

As had happened with the vintage Bentleys, heavier coachwork damaged the performance of the 3¹/₂ litre. Fortunately a more powerful engine was available by 1936, in the shape of the 4257 cc unit used in the new Rolls-Royce 25/30. This gave about an extra 16 bhp (then, as now, Rolls-Royce did not disclose the outputs of their engines), so performance was about the same as from the early 3¹/₂s: 90 mph (145 km/h) with reasonable coachwork. In 1938 the 4¹/₄ was given an over-drive top gear to cater for the new *Autobahnen*; this meant that at 90 mph the engine was turning at about 1500 rpm less than with the ordinary top gear. Production of the 4¹/₄ litre was 1241, slightly more than the 3¹/₂, which found 1191 customers.

The final prewar Bentley was the Mark V, which had the Rolls-Royce Wraith's coil independent front suspension and synchromesh on second as well as the higher gear ratios. Introduced in the summer of

One of the rare Mark Vs, of which only nineteen were made, this carries a Park Ward saloon body which clearly anticipates the post-war Mark VI.

Eddie Hall's 1934 TT car. This body was by Abbott but was soon transferred to a new chassis; because this work was done by Offord & Sons, it has been stated that they were the bodybuilders. This body was never used for racing, Hall using lighter bodies and, in 1936, a 4¹/₄ litre chassis.

1939, it was killed by the war; estimates of production vary between eleven and twenty. Probably seventeen were built with traditional styling (Park Ward saloon or drophead) and two of the Corniche streamlined saloon.

Rolls-Royce did not officially support Bentleys in racing, though they gave some aid to Eddie Hall's private entry of a light-weight 3¹/₂ litre in the 1934 Tourist Trophy, in which he finished second. He repeated this in 1935, and again in 1936 with a 4¹/₄ litre engine in the same car with a lighter body. Hall's was the fastest car on the circuit each year but lost out on handicap to the smaller-engined MGs and Rileys. After the war he ran the Bentley at Le Mans, finishing eighth in 1950.

Hall's 4¹/₄ litre TT car in the form in which it was raced at Le Mans in 1950. Hall finished eighth, two places behind the Embiricos Bentley.

20

'The Scalded Cat', an experimental car used by various Rolls-Royce staff members during the Second World War. It had the 5.6 litre straight-eight version of the B series engines, presumably in a Mark V chassis. Prince Philip tried it in 1949 and was said to have been reluctant to hand it back. His enthusiasm may have influenced Princess Elizabeth to choose a similarly powered Rolls-Royce Phantom IV in 1950, the first of a series of Rolls-Royces which soon ousted Daimlers as the official royal cars.

POSTWAR SUCCESS AND DECLINE

After the Second World War Bentleys became increasingly similar to Rolls-Royce cars, with a change to a more individual identity coming only in the 1980s. The parent company had moved from Derby to a factory at Crewe which had been built in 1938 for aero-engine construction, and this factory also incorporated a body plant. Here four-door saloon bodies made by Pressed Steel at Cowley, Oxford, were finished. Originally only Bentleys were fitted with these bodies, but from 1949 they also became available on the Rolls-Royce Silver Dawn. The decision to introduce a standard body was partly due to the high cost of custom coachwork, but also because the cars were aimed at export markets more than previously, and the traditional ash frame with aluminium panels was not suitable for some climates.

Announced in the spring of 1946, the postwar Bentley was called the Mark VI and shared with the Rolls-Royce Silver Wraith a new six-cylinder engine whose dimensions were the same as the Mark V/ Wraith, but it had a new valve layout, overhead inlet and side exhaust valves. This engine was part of a range called the B engines, made in four-, six- and eight-cylinder versions. The last was used in the Rolls-Royce Phantom IV and in an experimental Bentley nicknamed the 'Scalded Cat'. The six used in the Mark VI differed somewhat from that in the Silver Wraith, having twin SU carburetters in place of a single Stromberg, and a higher-lift camshaft.

About 80 per cent of the 5201 Mark VI chassis made between 1946 and 1952 had Pressed Steel bodies, but there were also numerous custom styles made. In the ten years after the Second World War British coachbuilders became virtually extinct, but before they disappeared they built many magnificent examples on both Bentley and Rolls-Royce. At least fourteen firms in Britain worked on the Mark VI, as well as some continental coachbuilders such as Franay, Saoutchik and Pininfarina. From mid 1951 the engine was enlarged to 4566 cc, and the Mark VI's successor, known as the R-type, came in 1952. The body was much the same but had a larger luggage boot, and automatic transmission was optional.

One of the most beautiful Bentleys ever made, the R-type Continental fastback

A 1948 Mark VI standard steel saloon, which accounted for about 80 per cent of all Mark VIs made. The bodies were built by Pressed Steel to Rolls-Royce's designs and finished off at the Crewe body works.

coupé, came out in 1952. Although the body was built by H. J. Mulliner, it was styled by a Rolls-Royce man, J. P. Blatchley, and offered as a standard model. The modifications from a standard R-type were the work of Ivan Evernden, who had been instructed that the car was to have a top speed of 120 mph (190 km/h). The compression ratio was raised and output increased, though Rolls-Royce have never divulged by how much. Not too much performance could be gained by tuning, if the traditional Bentley smoothness and silence were to be preserved, but Evernden and Blatchley were able to make considerable progress through lighter weight and better aerodynamics. Originally earmarked for export only, the R-type Continental cost £4890, when a standard saloon could be had for £3100.

Although the Mulliner coupé was the best-known, and most attractive, body built on the R-type Continental chassis, some bodies were made by Abbott, Park Ward, Graber and Pininfarina. Of the

Before the advent of specialised rally machinery, cars of the Bentley calibre were not infrequently seen in the Monte Carlo Rally. Mike Couper was the most successful with his Mark VI saloon, but here is a James Young two-door saloon leaving Paris during the 1954 event.

Three of the special bodies built on the Mark VI chassis. (Top) A rather formal razor-edge saloon which might look better with a Rolls-Royce radiator. (Centre) An H. J. Mulliner saloon with sweeping wing lines; Freestone & Webb built a very similar design. (Bottom) One of the few efforts by Continental coachbuilders, a coupé by Pininfarina.

The production R-type Continental, marketed from 1952 to 1955. The last cars had the larger 4887 cc engine. Automatic transmission was available, but manual boxes were more popular. Right-hand-drive Continentals had right-hand gear levers; left-hand-drive models had steering-column control.

One of the last custom-bodied Bentleys, a Hooper saloon on a 1956 S1 chassis. This design was also seen on the Rolls-Royce Silver Wraith.

The introduction of the S-type standard steel saloon brought a rapid drop in the output of chassis for special coachwork. Bentleys and Rolls-Royces were now identical apart from the radiator. This is a 1961 S2 with the 6.2 litre V8 engine.

A lightweight fastback coupé by H. J. Mulliner on a 1950 Mark VI chassis. It is an interesting car in that it clearly foreshadows the famous R-type Continental, also by Mulliner, which was announced two years later.

208 chassis, 193 had Mulliner bodies.

In April 1955 the R-type gave way to the S-type, whose Rolls-Royce equivalent was called the Silver Cloud. Engine capacity went up to 4887 cc and there was a new body from Pressed Steel, longer and wider, with wings flowing into the doors. There was now no difference between Bentley and Rolls-Royce versions except for the latter's traditional radiator, for which customers paid an additional £130. The Continental was continued on the S-type, with coupés by Mulliner and Park Ward, and a convertible by Park Ward. By 1959 the six-cylinder engine, whose ancestry dated back to the Rolls-Royce Twenty of 1922, had reached the limit of its development, but more power was needed if the cars were to keep up with the larger American cars. The answer was a completely new V8 of 6230 cc, the largest used in a Bentley since the 8 litre. Yet it was 10 pounds (4.5 kg) lighter than the six, owing to the light alloy cylinder block, and, with the same body as the S1, the new S2 was 15 mph (34 km/h) faster.

An unusually flamboyant design of 1957, a two-seater by Freestone & Webb. This style, with fins of almost Cadillac proportions, was also made on the Rolls chassis, just one of each. When photographed in the 1960s, the Bentley was owned by the estate agent Roy Brooks, celebrated for his unconventional advertisements.

The H. J. Mulliner Continental was continued on the S-type, though most people would prefer the lightness of the earlier design. This is a 1963 S3 version.

The engine remained largely unchanged until 1970, when it was enlarged to its present size of 6750 cc.

Twinned headlamps came on the S3 of 1962, and special models were still available, such as the Continental coupé or convertible by H. J. Mulliner and Park Ward, who merged in 1961, or the Flying Spur four-door saloon, also by Mulliner. After the introduction of the S3 there was no longer any difference in engine specification between the Continental and other Bentleys. The last Continental chassis was delivered to the coachbuilder on 20th November 1965 and was not received by the customer until January 1966, four months after the model had been officially replaced by the T series.

INTEGRAL CONSTRUCTION

In October 1965 all Bentleys and Rolls-Royces gave way to a new four-door saloon with integral construction and self-levelling independent suspension. Known as the Bentley T-type or Rolls-Royce Silver Shadow, it had been under development for nearly ten years, the first prototype running in 1957. Its design reflected changing tastes, for customers wanted a car with a lower profile, both figuratively and literally: one that yielded nothing in quality to its predecessors yet was less obviously a display of the owner's wealth. At least that was the reasoning, but it must be open to doubt because the T-series was outsold by ten to one by the Silver Shadow, the more ostentatious car

For those who wanted four doors and greater space in the rear compartment, H. J. Mulliner/ Park Ward offered the Flying Spur version of the Continental, seen here in S3 form for 1963.

1961 and 1963 versions of the S-type Continental Mulliner/Park Ward convertible. Both had V8 engines. Apart from the twinned headlamps, improvements on the 1963 S3 models included greater power assistance to the steering.

The integral construction of the T series precluded the variety of custom coachwork, but for a short time after its introduction in 1965 James Young offered this two-door saloon version. Only fifteen were made.

if only because of its Rolls radiator. The T-Type was 5 inches (127 mm) lower, 7 inches (178 mm) shorter and 3½ inches (89 mm) narrower than the S3. It was a very complex car, particularly in its self-levelling suspension. To keep the car on an even keel whatever the load, there was a hydraulically operated height-control system driven by the engine. When pass-engers entered the car or the boot was loaded with luggage, the level was quickly regained, at the rate of about half an inch (13 mm) per second. The work was carried out by four hydraulic pistons, those at the rear having a travel of 3 inches (76 mm). This was seldom fully utilised unless five heavy passengers and a full complement of luggage were being carried.

The Corniche was introduced in 1971 as an improved version of the Mulliner/Park Ward coupé and convertible, with engines giving about 10 per cent more power than the saloons. Bentley Corniches were always rarer than their Rolls-Royce equivalents, production from 1971 to 1984 being about 69 coupés and eighty convertibles. This is a 1977 convertible, with a standard four-door saloon behind it.

The Turbo R brought new standards of handling to the Bentley range. Major changes to suspension, wider tyres, alloy wheels and an air dam distinguished it from the regular Mulsannes.

REVIVAL IN THE 1980s

The T series years were very lean ones for the Bentley marque. In the early post-war years the Mark VI outsold the Rolls-Royces by three to one, but in the 1970s fewer than 10 per cent of the cars carried Bentley badges, and in 1980 the figure dropped to 4 per cent. It seemed hardly economic to perpetuate the name, but company changes and a new model led to a remarkable revival. After the collapse of Rolls-Royce Ltd in 1971, due to problems in the aero-engine side of the business, the cars were hived off and were built by a new company, Rolls-Royce Motors Ltd, under the direction of David Plastow, the former sales director of the car division. In August 1980 Rolls-Royce Motors became part of the Vickers Group, which was headed by David Plastow. The new head of Rolls-Royce Motors was George Fenn, who oversaw the introduction of a new model in the autumn of 1980. Before Plastow had moved to Vickers it had been decided that with the new model the Bentley profile would be raised, and this was symbolised by a name rather than a letter series. The Bentley was the Mulsanne, named after the Mulsanne straight at Le Mans, harking

back to the days of the Bentley Boys, while the Rolls-Royce was the Silver Spirit.

The new cars were styled by the Austrian-born Fritz Feller and had a heavier look than that of the T Series, giving the impression of more car for the money. The bodies were 2.3 inches (58 mm) wider, 2.9 inches (74 mm) longer and 1.3 inches (33 mm) lower, but more noticeable was a 30 per cent increase in window area. The engine was the same 6.7 litre V8 of the previous models.

In the spring of 1982 came a high-performance model which was to begin the process of distancing Bentley from Rolls-Royce. This was the Mulsanne Turbo, which used a Garrett AiResearch turbocharger to give a boost in power of about 50 per cent, from 200 to 300 bhp. Top speed was limited to 135 mph (217 km/h) by a sensor which restricted turbo boost, but acceleration from 0 to 60 mph (97 km/h) took only 7½ seconds, no mean feat for a car which weighed 4950 pounds (2245 kg). The Turbo's body was similar to that of the Mulsanne, but it could be easily identified by the radiator shell, which was painted in the same colour as

29

The Bentley Eight was a simplified version of the Mulsanne. Introduced in 1984, it is readily identified by its mesh grille. Priced at £49,497 on introduction, it cost £84,867 by the spring of 1992 but still undercut the Mulsanne by more than £7300.

the rest of the body, instead of silver. The makers were adamant that the Turbo would never carry a Rolls-Royce radiator, and it has been calculated that if it did it would need an additional 35 bhp to achieve the same performance, because of the drag imposed by the square radiator shell.

In 1985 the Turbo was joined by an improved model, the Turbo R, with modified suspension and larger tyres. The anti-roll bars were stiffened, and roll stiffness was increased at the rear by hydraulic restriction between the self-levelling units. The range was completed by a 'cheaper' Bentley, the Eight, with less luxurious interior and mesh radiator grille. Its price in 1984 was £49,497, or £5943 less than a Mulsanne and £12,246 less than a Mulsanne Turbo.

The sporting image of the new Bentleys

resulted in a dramatic improvement in sales. In 1986, when the group sold 2603 cars, the ratio between Rolls and Bentley was 60:40, and in 1991, with lower overall sales of 1731, the ratio was approximately 50:50.

The three models, Eight, Mulsanne and Turbo R, made up the Bentley range in 1992, joined by a new and more individual coupé, the Continental R. The letter designation was chosen as an evocation of the R-type Continental of the 1950s, and the new car is in the same spirit, a limited-production, higher-performance car sold at a price considerably above that of the saloons. The four-seater coupé body was designed by Ken Greenley and John Heffernan and was derived from a show car of 1985 called the Project 90. The engine was slightly tweaked to give greater power and torque, output now be-

In order to separate the Bentley from Rolls-Royce, the company showed a two-door coupé at the 1985 Geneva Show. Named Project 90, it was styled by John Heffernan and Ken Greenley, and the mock-up was built by IAD at Worthing. In the background is an R-type Continental, which Project 90 was intended to evoke.

ing an estimated 333 bhp. A four-speed General Motors automatic gearbox replaced the three-speeder of other models, though all Rolls-Royces and Bentleys received the four-speed box in the spring of 1992. The Continental R was priced at £175,000, which came down to £168,294 after the March 1992 budget (a Turbo R listed for £129,604), and production was limited to three hundred *per annum*. Two years' production had already been sold before the first examples were delivered, and some orders were placed only on the sight of photographs.

In September 1992 there arrived a new variant called the Brooklands. Priced at £91,489, it replaced the Eight and the Mulsanne S and featured a new bonnet and green badge harking back to the vintage Green Label Bentleys, new air dam and alloy wheels. Inside, the electric column-mounted gearchange was moved to the floor.

The future of Bentley is tied up with that of Rolls-Royce Motors, whose overall sales have been badly hit by the recession. At the time of writing there is a strong likelihood that Vickers will sell Rolls-Royce, but it is to be hoped that, whatever happens, the name of Bentley will still remain on one of Britain's finest cars.

Appropriately launched at the Brooklands Museum, the Bentley Brooklands is seen here on the banking with a 1930 Speed Six.

FURTHER READING

Many books have been written on Bentleys, but among the most valuable and definitive are the following:

Bastow, Donald. *W. O. Bentley, Engineer.* Haynes, 1978.
Bentley, W. O. *W. O., An Autobiography.* Hutchinson, 1958.
Bentley, W. O. *The Cars in My Life.* Hutchinson, 1961. An expanded version of the above.
Berthon, Darrell. *A Racing History of the Bentley.* Bodley Head, 1956.
Ellman-Brown, Michael. *Bentley, The Silent Sports Car 1931-1941.* Dalton Watson, 1989.
Fletcher, A. F. Rivers. *Bentleys Past and Present.* Gentry Books, 1982.
Frostick, Michael. *From Cricklewood to Crewe.* Osprey, 1980.
Green, Johnnie. *Bentley, Fifty Years of the Marque.* Dalton Watson, 1969.
Hay, Michael. *The Vintage Bentley 1919-1931.* Dalton Watson, 1986.
Nagle, Elizabeth. *The Other Bentley Boys.* Harrap, 1964. About the racing mechanics.
Sedgwick, Stanley. *All the Pre-war Bentleys, as New.* Bentley Drivers Club, 1976.
Steel, Rodney. *Bentley, the Cars from Crewe.* Dalton Watson, 1988.
Young, Hugh (compiler). *The Bentley Bedside Book.* Bentley Drivers' Club, 1961. Hardly definitive, but a fascinating pot-pourri of reminiscences and little-known facts.

PLACES TO VISIT

Bentley cars can be seen in a number of museums, including those listed here, but museum displays may be altered and readers are advised to telephone before travelling to check that relevant items are on show, as well as to find out the opening times.

Bentley Motor Museum, The Pump House, Bentley Farm, Halland, Lewes, East Sussex. Telephone: 0825 840574.

Brooklands Museum, The Clubhouse, Brooklands Road, Weybridge, Surrey KT13 0QN. Telephone: 0932 857381.

Donington Collection, Donington Park, Castle Donington, Derby DE7 2RP. Telephone: 0332 810048.

Doune Motor Museum, Carse of Cambus, Doune, Perthshire FK16 6HD. Telephone: 0786 841203.

Glasgow Museum of Transport, Kelvin Hall, 1 Bunhouse Road, Glasgow G3 8PZ. Telephone: 041-357 3929.

Haynes Sparkford Motor Museum, Sparkford, Yeovil, Somerset BA22 7LH. Telephone: 0963 40804.

Jersey Motor Museum, St Peter's Village, Jersey, Channel Islands JE3 7AG. Telephone: 0534 482966.

Manx Motor Museum, Crosby, Isle of Man. Telephone: 0624 851236.

Myreton Motor Museum, Aberlady, Longniddry, East Lothian EH32 0PZ. Telephone: 08757 288.

National Motor Museum, John Montagu Building, Beaulieu, Brockenhurst, Hampshire SO42 7ZN. Telephone: 0590 612345.

Peter Black Collection, Lawkholme Lane, Keighley, West Yorkshire BD21 3JQ. Telephone: 0535 661177.

Totnes Motor Museum, Steamer Quay, Totnes, Devon TQ9 5AL. Telephone: 0803 862777.

SOCIETIES
Vintage Bentleys can regularly be seen in action at meetings of the following clubs. Dates of meetings can be obtained from the secretaries.

Bentley Drivers' Club: W. J. Port, 16 Chearsley Road, Long Crendon, Aylesbury, Buckinghamshire HP18 9AW. Telephone: 0844 208233.

Vintage Sports Car Club: David Franklin, 121 Russell Road, Newbury, Berkshire RG14 5JX. Telephone: 0635 580612.

Project 90 was shown with the intention of assessing general reaction and opinions. These were clearly favourable as the company went ahead with the car, which appeared as the Continental R.